Collins

PRACTICE MULTIPLE CHOICE QUESTIONS

CAPE®
Economics

Dave Ramsingh

Collins

HarperCollins Publishers Ltd
The News Building
1 London Bridge Street
London SE1 9GF

First edition 2017

10 9 8 7 6 5 4 3 2

ISBN 978-0-00-822204-8

www.collins.co.uk/caribbeanschools

A catalogue record for this book is available from the British Library.

Typeset by QBS Learning
Printed and bound by CPI Group (UK) Ltd, Croydon, CR0 4YY

Author: Dave Ramsingh
Publisher: Elaine Higgleton
Commissioning Editor: Ben Gardiner
Managing Editor: Sarah Thomas
Project Manager: Alissa McWhinnie
Copy Editor: Kay Hawkins
Proofreader: Stephen York
Answer Checker: Julie Jackson
Artwork: QBS Learning
Cover design: Kevin Robbins and Gordon MacGilp
Production: Lauren Crisp
Additional Research: Curtis Ramkissoon, Damian Boodoo Spiedres, Smikveld Ramsingh

Contents

Download answers for free at www.collins.co.uk/caribbeanschools

Structure of the CAPE® Economics Paper 1 Examination

There are **45 questions** in the **Unit 1** examination; and **45 questions** in the **Unit 2** examination. The duration of each examination is **1½ hours**. The papers are worth **30%** of your final examination mark.

The Paper 1 examinations test the following core areas of the syllabus.

Unit 1: Microeconomics

Section	Number of Questions
Module 1: Methodology: Demand and Supply	15
Module 2: Market Structure, Market Failure and Intervention	15
Module 3: Distribution Theory	15
Total	**45**

Unit 2: Macroeconomics

Section	Number of Questions
Module 1: Models of the Macroeconomy	15
Module 2: Macroeconomic Problems and Policies	15
Module 3: Growth, Sustainable Development and Global Relations	15
Total	**45**

The questions test two profiles, **knowledge and comprehension**, and **use of knowledge**. Questions will be presented in a variety of ways including the use of diagrams, data, graphs, prose or other stimulus material.

Each question is allocated 1 mark. You will <u>not</u> lose a mark if a question is answered incorrectly.

Examination Tips

General strategies for answering multiple choice questions

- Read every word of each question very carefully and make sure you understand exactly what it is asking. Even if you think that the question appears simple or straightforward, there may be important information you could easily omit, especially small, but very important words such as *all* or *only*.

- When faced with a question that seems unfamiliar, re-read it very carefully. Underline or circle the key pieces of information provided. Re-read it again if necessary to make sure you are very clear as to what it is asking and that you are not misinterpreting it.

- Each question has four options, **A, B, C** and **D**, and only one is the correct answer. Look at all the options very carefully as the differences between them may be very subtle; never stop when you come across an option you think is the one required. Cross out options that you know are definitely incorrect. There may be two options that appear very similar; identify the difference between the two so you can select the correct answer.

- You have approximately two minutes per question. Some questions can be answered in less than one minute while other questions may require longer because of the reasoning or calculation involved. Do not spend too long on any one question.

- If a question appears difficult, place a mark, such as an asterisk, on your answer sheet alongside the question number and return to it when you have finished answering all the other questions. Remember to carefully remove the asterisk, or other markings, from the answer sheet using a good clean eraser as soon as you have completed the question.

- Answer every question. Marks are not deducted for incorrect answers. Therefore, it is in your best interest to make an educated guess in instances where you do not know the answer. Never leave a question unanswered.

- Always ensure that you are shading the correct question number on your answer sheet. It is very easy to make a mistake, especially if you plan on returning to skipped questions.

- Some questions may ask which of the options is NOT correct or is INCORRECT. Pay close attention to this because it is easy to fail to see the words *NOT* or *INCORRECT* and answer the question incorrectly.

- Some questions may give two or more answers that could be correct and you are asked to determine which is the *BEST* or *MOST LIKELY*. You must consider each answer very carefully before making your choice because the differences between them may be very subtle.

- When a question gives three or four answers numbered **I, II** and **III** or **I, II, III** and **IV**, one or more of these answers may be correct. You will then be given four combinations as options, for example:

  (A) I only

  (B) I and II only

  (C) II and III only

  (D) I, II and III

  Place a tick by all the answers that you think are correct before you decide on the final correct combination.

- Do not make any assumptions about your choice of options; just because two answers in succession have been **C**, it does not mean that the next one cannot be **C** as well.

- Try to leave time at the end of the examination to check over your answers, but never change an answer until you have thought about it again very carefully.

- A silent, non-programmable calculator is allowed in the examination. You are required to provide your own calculator. Since the different brands of calculators have unique features, it is advisable to take a calculator you are familiar with.

- You may be required to do simple calculations in the Paper 1 examinations. Be very careful and accurate when performing calculations. It is very easy to make an error and there may be an incorrect option similar to your calculation. For questions requiring you to perform a calculation, work out the answer before you look at the four options. Do this by writing your working on the question paper. If you do not find your answer in the options, you can then go back and recheck your workings for mistakes.

- Some questions are accompanied by diagrams, graphs, tables or prose. Read and inspect these carefully and use them to derive the best option for the question. You may make your own sketches to help you answer the questions.

Unit 1: Microeconomics

1 Which of the following BEST defines the concept of 'scarcity'?

(A) Goods and services to consumers are fixed in quantity   Ⓐ

(B) Resources allocated to production are not replaced   Ⓑ

(C) Unlimited human wants exceed the economy's limited resources   Ⓒ

(D) The wants of society are greater than the supply of goods   Ⓓ

2 A welder can make any combination of two products as shown in the table below.

Gates	Window Frames
75	12
60	15

What is the opportunity cost of making one window frame?

(A) 1 gate   Ⓐ

(B) 5 gates   Ⓑ

(C) 7 gates   Ⓒ

(D) 8 gates   Ⓓ

3 Which of the following statements most accurately defines a 'production possibility frontier'?

(A) The limit of the combinations of goods and services that can be produced in a country   Ⓐ

(B) The total quantity of goods and services that a country is likely to produce   Ⓑ

(C) The combination of goods and services that are desired by a country   Ⓒ

(D) A graph representing an economy producing goods and services for its citizens   Ⓓ

4 A combination of output that is within the production possibility frontier indicates

(A) Productive efficiency   Ⓐ

(B) Productive inefficiency   Ⓑ

(C) A minimum efficient scale of production   Ⓒ

(D) Pareto efficient production   Ⓓ

5 A production possibility frontier that is bowed outwards indicates

(A) A discovery of new resources   Ⓐ

(B) Increasing opportunity costs   Ⓑ

(C) Diminishing opportunity costs   Ⓒ

(D) Constant opportunity costs   Ⓓ

6 A production possibility frontier that is a straight line and downward sloping indicates

(A) Increasing opportunity costs   Ⓐ

(B) Decreasing opportunity costs   Ⓑ

(C) An absence of opportunity costs   Ⓒ

(D) Constant opportunity costs   Ⓓ

7 Which of the following situations is MOST likely to result when there are limited resources?

(A) Citizens are forced to make choices   Ⓐ

(B) The wealthy citizens will control all of the resources in the country   Ⓑ

(C) Many firms will be forced to cease operations   Ⓒ

(D) Individuals of lesser means would become poorer   Ⓓ

8 In one day a baker can produce EITHER 10 loaves of bread, which are sold at $5.00 each, or 20 cakes, which are sold at $1.00 each. The opportunity cost of the baker staying at home for three days is

(A) 10 loaves and 20 cakes   Ⓐ

(B) 30 loaves and 60 cakes   Ⓑ

(C) $210   Ⓒ

(D) $150   Ⓓ

<u>Item **9**</u> refers to the following diagrams illustrating four types of production possibility frontiers.

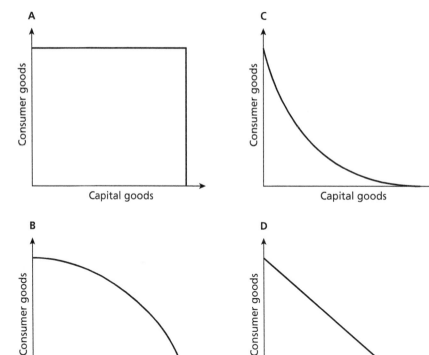

9 Which diagram illustrates decreasing opportunity costs: A, B, C or D?

     Ⓐ

     Ⓑ

     Ⓒ

     Ⓓ

Item **10** refers to the production possibility frontier shown below.

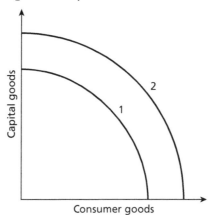

10 In this economy, a rightward equidistant shift of the curve from 1 to 2 illustrates the effects of

(A) Economic development   Ⓐ

(B) Economic growth   Ⓑ

(C) Constant returns   Ⓒ

(D) Recession   Ⓓ

11 Which of the following is an example of an economic normative statement?

(A) A recession in the United States will cause a reduction in tourist arrivals   Ⓐ

(B) A rise in the prices of basic food items will cause hardship to low income earners   Ⓑ

(C) The government should subsidise basic food items to protect low income earners   Ⓒ

(D) Free tertiary education will increase student enrolment at the University of the West Indies   Ⓓ

12 Which of the following is an advantage of a planned economy?

(A) Social costs and benefits influence economic decision-making   Ⓐ

(B) Planned economies promote competition   Ⓑ

(C) Resources are allocated by market forces   Ⓒ

(D) Prices are determined by market forces   Ⓓ

13 Which of the following is a disadvantage of a planned economy?

(A) Bureaucratic decision-making (A)

(B) Consumers choose too many demerit goods (B)

(C) Competition among firms increases the prices of resources (C)

(D) Overproduction of goods and services (D)

14 Which of the following is a distinguishing feature of a mixed economy?

(A) Private citizens can own stock in all state enterprises (A)

(B) Imported goods are not subject to taxation (B)

(C) The private and state sectors coexist to provide goods and services for all citizens (C)

(D) All aspects of the economy are controlled by the government (D)

15 Prices are determined in a mixed economy by

(A) The government only (A)

(B) Producers, consumers and the government (B)

(C) Producers and consumers only (C)

(D) Market forces only (D)

1 The price elasticity of demand for Good X is 0.5. If the price of the good changes by 20%, what is the corresponding percentage change in quantity demanded?

(A) 10% Ⓐ

(B) 20% Ⓑ

(C) 5% Ⓒ

(D) 15% Ⓓ

2 The price elasticity of demand for Good X is perfectly elastic. 25 units are sold at $3.00 per unit. If the price is raised to $5.00, total expenditure on Good X will be

(A) $250.00 Ⓐ

(B) $75.00 Ⓑ

(C) $300.00 Ⓒ

(D) $0.00 Ⓓ

3 The price elasticity of demand for a good is unitary. When the price of the good is $2.00, the quantity demanded is 40 units. If the price of the good increases to $4.00, what will be the change in quantity demanded?

(A) 24 Ⓐ

(B) 20 Ⓑ

(C) No change Ⓒ

(D) 80 Ⓓ

4 The price elasticity of demand for a good is unitary. What will decrease if the price is increased?

(A) Total revenue Ⓐ

(B) Expenditure on substitutes Ⓑ

(C) Quantity demanded Ⓒ

(D) Expenditure on complements Ⓓ

5 The mid-point of a linear demand curve has a price elasticity of demand which is

(A) Inelastic   Ⓐ

(B) Very elastic   Ⓑ

(C) Unitary   Ⓒ

(D) Zero elastic   Ⓓ

6 A normal good is one which is

(A) Subject to a negative income effect   Ⓐ

(B) Subject to a positive income effect   Ⓑ

(C) Subject to an extreme negative income effect   Ⓒ

(D) Does not respond to price changes   Ⓓ

7 An inferior good is one which is

(A) Subject to a negative income effect   Ⓐ

(B) Subject to a positive income effect   Ⓑ

(C) Subject to an extreme negative income effect   Ⓒ

(D) Has a demand curve that is upward sloping   Ⓓ

8 Which of the following best explains the term 'indifference curve'?

(A) A curve which represents a budget line   Ⓐ

(B) A curve which links price to quantity demanded   Ⓑ

(C) A curve which shows the same levels of satisfaction   Ⓒ

(D) A curve which shows different combinations of two goods that yield the same level of satisfaction   Ⓓ

9 Which of the following factors would cause a change in demand for a good?

(A) A change in price   (A)

(B) A change in the cost of the good   (B)

(C) A change in real income   (C)

(D) A change in indirect taxes   (D)

10 One exogenous factor that would affect the demand for a pineapple is

(A) The quantity demanded   (A)

(B) The quantity supplied   (B)

(C) Income of the buyer   (C)

(D) The market price of the pineapple   (D)

<u>Item **11**</u> refers to the following table, which shows the prices and quantity demanded for beef and chicken, both before and after a change in the price of beef.

	Before		After	
Good	**Price ($)**	**Qd (kg)**	**Price ($)**	**Qd (kg)**
Beef	10.00	20	5.00	30
Chicken	4.00	12	4.00	9

11 In the above example, chicken and beef are substitutes. What is the cross-price elasticity of demand for chicken with respect to a change in the price of beef?

(A) −2   (A)

(B) −1/2   (B)

(C) +1/2   (C)

(D) +2   (D)

Items **12–13** refer to the following diagram, where XY is the consumer's initial budget line and ZW is the new budget line.

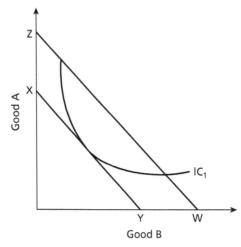

12 What has happened to cause the budget line to shift from XY to ZW?

(A) Consumer income and prices of both goods decreased   (A)

(B) Consumer income decreased and the prices of both goods increased   (B)

(C) Prices of Goods A and B fell by the same proportion   (C)

(D) Prices of Goods A and B increased by the same proportion   (D)

13 IC_1 is convex to the origin because

(A) Consumer opportunity cost is decreasing   (A)

(B) Consumer opportunity cost is increasing   (B)

(C) The marginal rate of substitution is decreasing   (C)

(D) The marginal rate of substitution is increasing   (D)

14 A positive change in consumer income will shift a downward sloping demand curve (*ceteris paribus*) in which direction?

(A) To the right   Ⓐ

(B) To the left   Ⓑ

(C) No change   Ⓒ

(D) In both directions   Ⓓ

Item **15** refers to the diagram below, showing the relationship between income and quantity demanded.

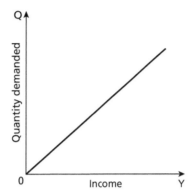

15 The diagram above BEST describes the relationship between income and quantity demanded of

(A) A Veblen good   Ⓐ

(B) A normal good   Ⓑ

(C) A merit good   Ⓒ

(D) An inferior good   Ⓓ

1 More is supplied at higher prices because

(A) High prices provide an incentive for producers to increase supply   (A)

(B) Raw materials are inelastic in supply   (B)

(C) Firms prefer to keep inventory for sudden changes in demand   (C)

(D) Demand for some goods increases with price   (D)

2 Which of the following will cause a shift of the supply curve downward and to the right?

(A) Changes in income   (A)

(B) Changes in taste, fashion and habit   (B)

(C) Changes in product promotion   (C)

(D) An increase in labour productivity   (D)

3 A long run production is governed by which law?

(A) The law of increasing average physical product   (A)

(B) The law of returns to scale   (B)

(C) The optimal purchase rule   (C)

(D) The law of diminishing marginal productivity   (D)

4 Diminishing returns are caused by

(A) Some factor inputs being more efficient than others   (A)

(B) An oversupply of the fixed factor in the production process   (B)

(C) Oversupply of the variable factor   (C)

(D) The average physical product falling below the marginal physical product   (D)

5 In the short run

(A) At least one fixed factor cannot be changed ⒜

(B) All fixed factors can be changed Ⓑ

(C) At least one variable factor cannot be changed Ⓒ

(D) The variable factors cannot be changed Ⓓ

6 If increasing amounts of a variable factor are added to a fixed quantity of a factor, the marginal product will initially rise but thereafter decline. This is a statement of

(A) The law of diminishing marginal utility ⒜

(B) The law of diminishing marginal returns Ⓑ

(C) The law of decreasing returns to scale Ⓒ

(D) The law of constant returns Ⓓ

7 In which order do TPP, MPP and APP begin to decrease in short run production?

NOTE. TPP = Total Physical Product; MPP = Marginal Physical Product; APP = Average Physical Product.

	1st	2nd	3rd	
(A)	APP	TPP	MPP	⒜
(B)	TPP	APP	MPP	Ⓑ
(C)	MPP	TPP	APP	Ⓒ
(D)	MPP	APP	TPP	Ⓓ

8 Which of the following is a factor that determines the elasticity of supply?

(A) Changes in income ⒜

(B) Spare capacity Ⓑ

(C) Indirect taxes Ⓒ

(D) Government subsidies Ⓓ

9 A car park filled to capacity has a price elasticity of supply that is

(A) Unitary   Ⓐ

(B) Perfectly inelastic   Ⓑ

(C) Perfectly elastic   Ⓒ

(D) Elastic   Ⓓ

10 The supply curve is unitary in elasticity when it

(A) Passes through the horizontal axis   Ⓐ

(B) Passes through the vertical axis   Ⓑ

(C) Passes through the point of origin   Ⓒ

(D) Is downward sloping   Ⓓ

11 An indirect tax causes the

(A) Supply curve to move upward and to the right   Ⓐ

(B) Demand curve to move downward and to the right   Ⓑ

(C) Supply curve to move upward and to the left   Ⓒ

(D) Demand curve to move upward and to the left   Ⓓ

12 The elasticity of supply is

(A) More elastic in the long run   Ⓐ

(B) More elastic in the short run   Ⓑ

(C) Less elastic in the long run   Ⓒ

(D) Inelastic in the long run   Ⓓ

13 A production function is defined as

(A) The rate at which inputs create output   Ⓐ

(B) The maximum output attainable from different combinations of inputs   Ⓑ

(C) The rate at which supply responds to changes in demand   Ⓒ

(D) The upward sloping supply curve   Ⓓ

14 Which of the following measures productivity?

(A) Output / Input per hour   Ⓐ

(B) Total input / Total output   Ⓑ

(C) Output per time period   Ⓒ

(D) Input / Output per day   Ⓓ

15 Which of the following measures production?

(A) Output / Input per week   Ⓐ

(B) Total cost / Total output   Ⓑ

(C) Total output per time period   Ⓒ

(D) Input / Output per day   Ⓓ

<u>Item 1</u> refers to the graph below which represents the market for an inter-island shuttle air service.

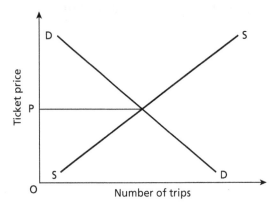

1 OP is the equilibrium price of the fare charged. If the government imposes a price ceiling to enable low income citizens to use the service, the price ceiling should be placed

(A) Above the equilibrium price OP

(B) Below the equilibrium price OP

(C) At the price OP

(D) Either above or below the price OP

(A)

(B)

(C)

(D)

<u>Item 2</u> refers to the diagram below, showing producer surplus.

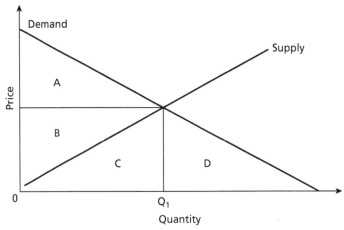

2 Producer surplus is represented by which area in the diagram above?

(A) The area to the left of the supply curve indicated by the letter B   Ⓐ

(B) The area to the right of the supply curve indicated by the letter C   Ⓑ

(C) The area above the price line indicated by the letter A   Ⓒ

(D) The area to the left of the demand curve indicated by the letter D   Ⓓ

3 A price floor is likely to

(A) Reduce consumer surplus   Ⓐ

(B) Reduce producer surplus   Ⓑ

(C) Increase consumer surplus   Ⓒ

(D) Leave producer surplus unchanged   Ⓓ

4 A fall in equilibrium price will cause

(A) A reduction in producer surplus   Ⓐ

(B) A reduction in consumer surplus   Ⓑ

(C) An increase in producer surplus   Ⓒ

(D) No change in consumer surplus   Ⓓ

5 Consumer surplus is equal to zero when

(A) The demand curve is perfectly elastic   Ⓐ

(B) The demand curve is perfectly inelastic   Ⓑ

(C) The supply curve is perfectly elastic   Ⓒ

(D) The supply curve is perfectly inelastic   Ⓓ

6 A price ceiling is likely to

(A) Increase producer surplus   Ⓐ

(B) Increase consumer surplus   Ⓑ

(C) Leave producer surplus unchanged   Ⓒ

(D) Reduce consumer surplus   Ⓓ

7 Which of the following is an example of a price ceiling?

(A) The government's price support for farmers   Ⓐ

(B) Rent controls   Ⓑ

(C) Value added taxes   Ⓒ

(D) The introduction of a minimum wage   Ⓓ

8 Which of the following is an example of a price floor?

(A) The government's price support for farmers   Ⓐ

(B) Rent controls   Ⓑ

(C) Value added taxes   Ⓒ

(D) The introduction of a minimum wage   Ⓓ

<u>Item **9**</u> refers to the diagram below for the price of goat meat when chicken is a close substitute.

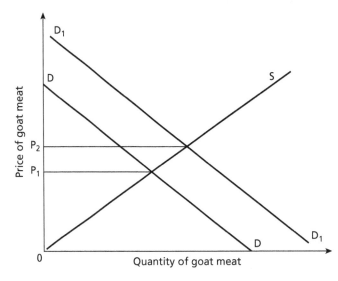

9 The change in price from P_1 to P_2 was MOST likely to have been caused by

(A) An increase in costs related to goat rearing   (A)

(B) An increase in the price of chicken   (B)

(C) An outbreak of an illness affecting goats   (C)

(D) An increase in a specific tax on goat meat   (D)

10 The demand for cellular phones increases while new technology reduces their cost. What will be the effect on the price of cellular phones and the quantity supplied?

	Price	Quantity
(A)	Fall	Decrease
(B)	Uncertain	Uncertain
(C)	Rise	Increase
(D)	Fall	Uncertain

(A)

(B)

(C)

(D)

11 Consumer surplus may be defined as

(A) The addition of total utility to total expenditure   (A)

(B) The equality of total utility to total expenditure   (B)

(C) The difference between total utility and total expenditure   (C)

(D) The excess of total spending over total utility   (D)

12 Which of the following are examples of a price floor?

    (I) Rent controls

    (II) Minimum wage

    (III) The addition of value added tax to prices of goods and services

    (IV) Farm price supports by the government

(A) I and IV only   (A)

(B) II and IV only   (B)

(C) I and II only   (C)

(D) II and III only   (D)

Item **13** refers to the diagram below which shows the effect of a specific tax.

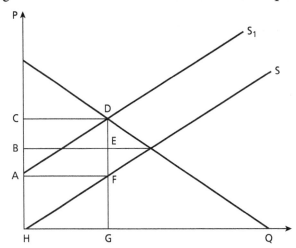

13 Which of the rectangles represents the burden of the tax on the consumer?

(A) ABEF

(B) ACDF

(C) BCDE

(D) HAFG

Ⓐ

Ⓑ

Ⓒ

Ⓓ

1.1.5 The Theory of Costs

1 Fixed costs of production

(A) Change as output increases

(B) Do not change as output changes

(C) Vary with profit

(D) Are unrelated to overhead costs

Ⓐ

Ⓑ

Ⓒ

Ⓓ

2 Which of the following is NOT affected by the fixed cost of production?

(A) Marginal cost   Ⓐ

(B) Average fixed cost   Ⓑ

(C) Average total cost   Ⓒ

(D) Total variable cost   Ⓓ

3 Marginal cost is BEST defined as

(A) The addition to average variable cost of producing one extra unit of output   Ⓐ

(B) The addition to total variable cost of producing one extra unit of output   Ⓑ

(C) The addition to total cost of producing one extra unit of output   Ⓒ

(D) The addition to total fixed cost of producing one extra unit of output   Ⓓ

4 A carnival band craftsman produces 10 costumes at an average cost of TT$3000 per costume. When he produces the 11th costume, the average cost falls to TT$2900. What is the marginal cost of the 11th costume?

(A) $1000   Ⓐ

(B) $600   Ⓑ

(C) $2400   Ⓒ

(D) $1900   Ⓓ

5 Diseconomies of scale begin when long run production is

(A) Before the minimum point on a U-shaped long run average cost curve   Ⓐ

(B) Beyond the minimum point on a U-shaped long run average cost curve   Ⓑ

(C) At the end of a rising U-shaped long run average cost curve   Ⓒ

(D) At the beginning of a long run average cost curve   Ⓓ

6 Marginal cost must mathematically intersect ATC and AVC at which point?

(A) Minimum ATC and AVC Ⓐ

(B) Before minimum AVC and ATC Ⓑ

(C) After minimum AVC and ATC Ⓒ

(D) Minimum AVC but beyond minimum ATC Ⓓ

7 Which of the following is an example of fixed costs?

(A) Interest paid on loans Ⓐ

(B) Weekly paid labour Ⓑ

(C) Electricity costs Ⓒ

(D) Raw material inputs Ⓓ

8 The point where marginal cost = average total cost indicates

(A) Decreasing returns to scale Ⓐ

(B) Diseconomies of scale Ⓑ

(C) Optimum output Ⓒ

(D) Equilibrium output Ⓓ

The following abbreviations apply to <u>Item **9**</u>.
APPL = Average physical product of labour; MPPL = Marginal physical product of labour;
APPK = Average physical product of capital; MPPK = Marginal physical product of capital;
PL = Price of labour; PK = Price of capital

9 The optimum factor combination for a firm which achieves the least cost would be

(A) APPK / PK = APPL / PL Ⓐ

(B) MPPL / PL = MPPK / PK Ⓑ

(C) MRPL / PL = MRPK / PK Ⓒ

(D) MPPL / PK = MPPK / PL Ⓓ

Item **10** refers to the diagram below, showing output against cost.

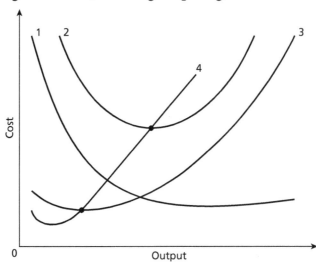

10 The curves labelled 1 and 4 represent

(A) Total fixed cost and average total cost   Ⓐ

(B) Average total cost and average variable cost   Ⓑ

(C) Total fixed cost and average variable cost   Ⓒ

(D) Average fixed cost and marginal cost   Ⓓ

11 Which of the following is an example of an internal economy of scale?

(A) Traffic congestion   Ⓐ

(B) Improvements in services infrastructure   Ⓑ

(C) Division of labour   Ⓒ

(D) The setting up of support services for firms in a location   Ⓓ

1 Normal profit is defined as

(A) The minimum level of profit necessary to ensure that existing firms remain in the industry   Ⓐ

(B) When total revenue is at a maximum   Ⓑ

(C) The maximum profit that is possible for the firm to achieve   Ⓒ

(D) When average revenue is greater than average cost of production   Ⓓ

The following abbreviations apply to <u>items 2–5</u>.
AR = Average Revenue; MC = Marginal Cost; MR = Marginal Revenue; AFC = Average Fixed Cost; ATC = Average Total Cost; AVC = Average Variable Cost.

2 Which of the following is true for all market structures?

(A) AR = Price = Demand   Ⓐ

(B) AR = MC = AVC   Ⓑ

(C) MR = AR = ATC   Ⓒ

(D) ATC = Price = MC   Ⓓ

3 Profit maximisation is represented by which of the following?

(A) AVC = AR   Ⓐ

(B) ATC = AVC   Ⓑ

(C) MC = MR   Ⓒ

(D) AFC = AR   Ⓓ

4 The short run supply curve of a competitive firm is indicated where

(A) ATC is above AVC   Ⓐ

(B) MC is above AVC   Ⓑ

(C) MC is above AFC   Ⓒ

(D) AR is above ATC   Ⓓ

5 Normal profit is indicated at an output level where

(A) ATC is greater than MC   (A)

(B) ATC = AR   (B)

(C) AR = MC   (C)

(D) AR is greater than ATC   (D)

6 A perfectly competitive firm making short run above normal profits can only make normal profits in the long run mainly due to

(A) Strong barriers to entry   (A)

(B) No barriers to entry   (B)

(C) Imperfect knowledge   (C)

(D) Imperfect mobility   (D)

7 The exit conditions of a firm require the firm to cover which of the following? LRAC = Long run average cost

(A) AVC   (A)

(B) ATC   (B)

(C) MC   (C)

(D) LRAC   (D)

<u>Item **8**</u> refers to the diagram below, showing perfect competition.

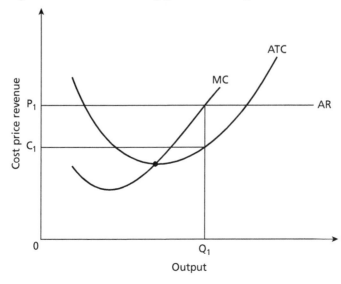

8 The diagram illustrates

(A) Perfect competition in the short run making a loss Ⓐ

(B) Perfect competition in the long run making normal profit Ⓑ

(C) Perfect competition making above normal profit in the short run Ⓒ

(D) Perfect competition making normal profit in the short run Ⓓ

9 When the average revenue curve of a firm is linear and downward sloping

(A) The marginal revenue is the same as average revenue Ⓐ

(B) The marginal revenue is less than average revenue and bisects the X axis Ⓑ

(C) The marginal revenue is greater than average revenue Ⓒ

(D) Average revenue is greater than marginal revenue Ⓓ

10 In the kinked demand curve of an oligopoly market structure

(A) AR is downward sloping and kinked while MR is discontinuous Ⓐ

(B) Both AR and MR are continuous and downward sloping Ⓑ

(C) AR is discontinuous while MR is a linear curve Ⓒ

(D) Both AR and MR are vertical Ⓓ

Items **11–12** refer to the diagram of a perfectly competitive firm in the short run.

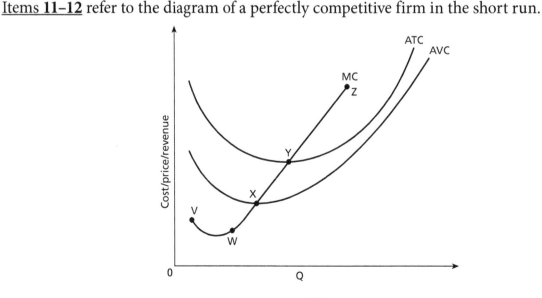

11 Which segment of the curve represents the short run supply curve of the firm?

(A) VW   Ⓐ

(B) WX   Ⓑ

(C) XY   Ⓒ

(D) XZ   Ⓓ

12 Which segment of the curve represents the long run supply curve of the firm?

(A) YZ   Ⓐ

(B) WZ   Ⓑ

(C) VY   Ⓒ

(D) WY   Ⓓ

13 All of the following factors determine the structure of a market EXCEPT

(A) The intervention of the government   Ⓐ

(B) The number of buyers and sellers in the industry   Ⓑ

(C) Barriers to entry and exit of firms in the industry   Ⓒ

(D) The ability of firms to set prices in the industry   Ⓓ

14 Using marginalism, the concept of the equilibrium output of all firms in all market structures is determined when

(A) Marginal Cost = Average Revenue   Ⓐ

(B) Marginal Cost = Marginal Revenue   Ⓑ

(C) Total Cost = Total Revenue   Ⓒ

(D) Marginal Cost = Total Revenue   Ⓓ

Items **15–18** refer to the diagram below of a profit maximising monopolist.

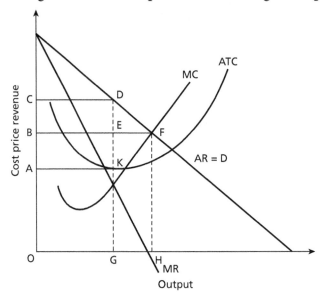

15 Which of the following rectangles represents the total costs of the firm at equilibrium output?

(A) OBFH   Ⓐ

(B) OCDG   Ⓑ

(C) OAKG   Ⓒ

(D) OBEG   Ⓓ

16 Which of the following rectangles represents the total revenue of the firm at equilibrium output?

(A) OBFH   Ⓐ

(B) OBEG   Ⓑ

(C) OAKG   Ⓒ

(D) OCDG   Ⓓ

17 Which of the following rectangles represents the profit of the firm at equilibrium output?

(A) ABEK

(B) BCDE

(C) ACDK

(D) OBEG

Ⓐ

Ⓑ

Ⓒ

Ⓓ

18 What level of profit is the firm making at equilibrium output?

(A) Normal profit

(B) Zero profit

(C) Loss

(D) Above normal profit

Ⓐ

Ⓑ

Ⓒ

Ⓓ

Items **19–21** refer to the diagram below of a market structure.

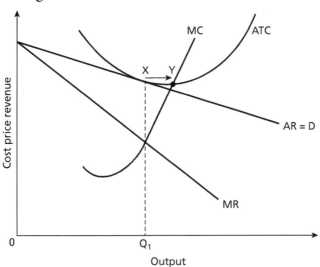

19 What market structure is represented by the diagram?

(A) Perfect competition in the short run

(B) Monopoly in the long run

(C) Monopoly in the short run

(D) Monopolistic competition in the long run

Ⓐ

Ⓑ

Ⓒ

Ⓓ

20 The tangency point at X was caused by

(A) AR moving upward and to the right   Ⓐ

(B) AR moving to the left and becoming more elastic   Ⓑ

(C) ATC moving upward and to the right   Ⓒ

(D) ATC moving downward and to the left as average cost fell   Ⓓ

21 Using marginalism, the concept of equilibrium output, points X to Y, is called

(A) Productivity zone   Ⓐ

(B) Diseconomies of scale   Ⓑ

(C) Decreasing returns to scale   Ⓒ

(D) Excess capacity   Ⓓ

<u>Item **22**</u> refers to the diagram of a monopoly.

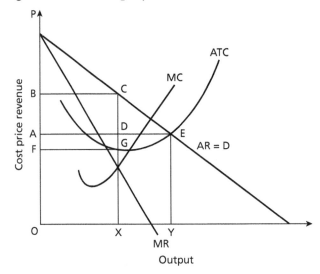

22 The monopolist has adjusted his output level from Y to a profit maximising output level X. The loss of consumer surplus from this change in output is represented by

(A) OAEY   Ⓐ

(B) PBC   Ⓑ

(C) ABCE   Ⓒ

(D) APE   Ⓓ

23 The demand curve of a monopolistic firm is different from a monopolist because

    (A) The demand curve of a monopolistic firm is more elastic   Ⓐ

    (B) The demand curve of a monopolistic firm is more inelastic   Ⓑ

    (C) The demand curve of a monopolist is more elastic   Ⓒ

    (D) The demand curve of a monopolist firm is perfectly elastic   Ⓓ

<u>Items **24–25**</u> refer to the diagram of short run costs and revenue of a perfectly competitive firm.

24 Point Z represents

    (A) Optimum output   Ⓐ

    (B) Equilibrium output   Ⓑ

    (C) The least cost combination   Ⓒ

    (D) Optimum and equilibrium output   Ⓓ

25 Assuming that a firm is earning above normal profits, at which point would marginal cost (MC) be equal to marginal revenue (MR)?

    (A) W   Ⓐ

    (B) X   Ⓑ

    (C) A   Ⓒ

    (D) Z   Ⓓ

26 Firms are more likely to collude in an oligopoly if

(A) Products are very different   (A)

(B) Products are not branded   (B)

(C) There are few firms who dominate the industry   (C)

(D) There is a sudden change in demand   (D)

27 Which of the following is NOT a model of oligopoly?

(A) Dominant price leader   (A)

(B) Barometric price leader   (B)

(C) Cartel   (C)

(D) Satisficer   (D)

28 Two measures of market concentration are

(A) The elasticity coefficient   (A)

(B) The retail market index   (B)

(C) Concentration ratio and Lorenz curve   (C)

(D) Concentration ratio and Herfindahl–Hirschman index   (D)

29 Three main features of an oligopoly are

(A) Price rigidity, interdependence and profit maximisation   (A)

(B) Price rigidity, interdependence and marginal cost pricing   (B)

(C) Price rigidity, interdependence and non-price competition   (C)

(D) Managerial utility, collusion and interdependence   (D)

Items **30–32** refer to the table below.

Firms	Market Share (%)
1	40
2	30
3	10
4	5
5	3
6	2

30 Calculate the percentage of the Five-Firm Concentration Ratio from the information in the table above.

(A) 5%   Ⓐ

(B) 90%   Ⓑ

(C) 88%   Ⓒ

(D) 24.1%   Ⓓ

31 Based on the calculation of the Herfindahl–Hirschman index from the information in the table above, this market may be described as

(A) Fairly concentrated   Ⓐ

(B) Highly concentrated   Ⓑ

(C) Not concentrated   Ⓒ

(D) Marginally concentrated   Ⓓ

32 The Herfindahl–Hirschman index of the six firms listed in the table is

(A) 170   Ⓐ

(B) 2638   Ⓑ

(C) 28 900   Ⓒ

(D) 5250   Ⓓ

33 Which of the following supports the kinked demand curve of an oligopoly?

    (A) Rival firms will match a price cut   Ⓐ

    (B) Rival firms will match a price increase   Ⓑ

    (C) Rival firm will not match a price cut or price increase   Ⓒ

    (D) Rival firms will match a price increase but not a price cut   Ⓓ

34 In the kinked demand theory of oligopoly

    (A) The upper portion of the demand curve is inelastic   Ⓐ

    (B) The downward portion of the demand curve is elastic   Ⓑ

    (C) The upward portion of the demand curve is elastic   Ⓒ

    (D) The demand curve has a discontinuous portion   Ⓓ

35 Which market structure would have a Herfindahl–Hirschman index of 10 000?

    (A) Perfect competition   Ⓐ

    (B) Natural oligopoly   Ⓑ

    (C) Pure monopoly   Ⓒ

    (D) Monopolistic competition   Ⓓ

1.2.2 Market Failure

1 Market failure occurs when

    (A) Profit maximisation is not achieved   Ⓐ

    (B) Social marginal benefit is not equal to social marginal cost   Ⓑ

    (C) Private marginal benefit is equal to social marginal benefit   Ⓒ

    (D) Private marginal cost is equal to social marginal cost   Ⓓ

2 Which of the following is NOT a cause of market failure?

(A) The non-provision of public goods by the free market   (A)

(B) Tradeable permits   (B)

(C) Externalities   (C)

(D) Monopoly   (D)

3 When people enjoy benefits without paying for them, this is known as

(A) The non-rival problem   (A)

(B) The non-rider problem   (B)

(C) The non-excludable problem   (C)

(D) The free-rider problem   (D)

4 A situation where consuming a unit of a good does NOT reduce the quantity available to others is called

(A) The non-excludable problem   (A)

(B) The non-rival problem   (B)

(C) The social benefit problem   (C)

(D) The private benefit problem   (D)

5 Which of the following may result when SMB < SMC?

NOTE. SMB = Social Marginal Benefit; SMC = Social Marginal Cost.

(A) Market failure   (A)

(B) Pareto efficiency   (B)

(C) Deadweight gain   (C)

(D) Loss of market share   (D)

6 Occupational immobility occurs when

   (A) There are barriers to taking up employment in a different region   Ⓐ

   (B) It is easy to take up employment in a different region   Ⓑ

   (C) There are barriers to taking up employment in a different occupation   Ⓒ

   (D) It is easy take up employment in a different occupation   Ⓓ

<u>Item 7</u> refers to the diagram below, showing marginal cost.

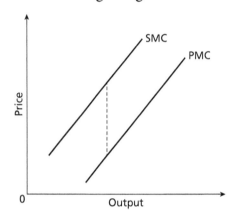

The following abbreviations apply to <u>Item 7</u>.
PMC = Private marginal cost; SMC = Social marginal cost

7 In the diagram, the vertical distance between PMC and SMC is referred to as

   (A) Excluded marginal cost   Ⓐ

   (B) Extra marginal cost   Ⓑ

   (C) External marginal cost   Ⓒ

   (D) Exceeded marginal cost   Ⓓ

8 The total social cost of smoking cigarettes is

   (A) The increased chances of non-smokers nearby contracting respiratory illnesses   Ⓐ

   (B) The marginal cost of producing one extra cigarette   Ⓑ

   (C) The opportunity cost of purchasing a cigarette   Ⓒ

   (D) The increased chances of non-smokers nearby contracting respiratory illnesses plus the private cost of producing the additional cigarette   Ⓓ

9 A situation is Pareto efficient if it is

(A) Possible to improve someone's position without doing harm to others   Ⓐ

(B) Impossible to make someone better off without negatively affecting others   Ⓑ

(C) Possible to make someone worse off and improve everyone else's position   Ⓒ

(D) Impossible to make anyone better off   Ⓓ

10 Asymmetric information occurs when one party in a transaction

(A) Has more information than the other party in the transaction   Ⓐ

(B) Has less information than other parties in the transaction   Ⓑ

(C) Is not aware he/she has more information than the other party   Ⓒ

(D) Has no information and the other party also has none   Ⓓ

11 Someone who purchases motor insurance and acts irresponsibly may cause

(A) Adverse selection   Ⓐ

(B) Moral hazard   Ⓑ

(C) Increased private benefit   Ⓒ

(D) Immoral hazard   Ⓓ

12 When a good can be provided to an additional person at zero cost the good is

(A) A private good   Ⓐ

(B) Normal   Ⓑ

(C) Non-rival   Ⓒ

(D) Non-excludable   Ⓓ

13 The concept of 'adverse selection' implies that

(A) Persons who have insurance may tend to be less careful and thus increase risks (A)

(B) Persons who take out insurance are those with the highest risk (B)

(C) Those who sell insurance policies are less well informed than those who buy them (C)

(D) Those who choose insurance policies often don't really need them (D)

14 The term deadweight loss can be BEST defined as

(A) Loss of profit for a firm in the short run (A)

(B) A combination of internal and external diseconomies of scale (B)

(C) A decrease in the net welfare to society (C)

(D) Loss of profit for a firm in the long run (D)

15 Deadweight loss is maximised when

(A) Total welfare is equal to zero (A)

(B) Total revenue is zero (B)

(C) Total cost is zero (C)

(D) Price = Marginal cost (D)

1 Which of the following is NOT an example of private sector intervention in the correction of market failure?

(A) Corporate code conduct which governs issues such as waste disposal and adherence to health and safety standards Ⓐ

(B) Social responsibility such as ensuring that marketed products are safe and providing multilingual information on safety and storage Ⓑ

(C) Company voluntary agreements are agreements that allow failing companies to renegotiate their debts to prevent insolvency and protect the interests of their clients Ⓒ

(D) The imposition of an indirect tax on producers Ⓓ

2 Two events, a block party and a 20 over cricket game cost exactly the same to organise. However, the 20 over cricket game gives twice as much enjoyment as the block party. If allocative efficiency is to exist, then

(A) Half as many block parties as 20 over cricket games should be staged Ⓐ

(B) Twice as many 20 over cricket games as block parties should be staged Ⓑ

(C) Twice as many block parties as 20 over cricket games should be staged Ⓒ

(D) The same number of block parties as 20 over cricket games should be staged Ⓓ

3 Which of the following BEST defines external cost?

(A) The opportunity cost of producing an additional unit of production Ⓐ

(B) The cost of producing an additional unit of a good or service Ⓑ

(C) The cost arising out of an activity that is imposed on non-participating third parties Ⓒ

(D) The cost of producing a good in a foreign country Ⓓ

4 An important characteristic of a private good is that

(A) The consumption of one unit does not reduce the quantity available to other persons Ⓐ

(B) Other persons cannot be excluded from consuming the good Ⓑ

(C) It is consumed by everyone equally Ⓒ

(D) The buyer of the good can exclude everyone from consuming the good Ⓓ

5 Which of the following types of intervention gives rise to 'Voluntary agreements'?

(A) Special interest groups Ⓐ

(B) Private sector Ⓑ

(C) Government Ⓒ

(D) The Ombudsman Ⓓ

6 A government grants a subsidy to encourage the consumption of Good A and at the same time imposes an indirect tax on Good B as a disincentive to consumption. Goods A and B can be classed as

	Good A	Good B
(A)	Demerit	Merit	Ⓐ
(B)	Public	Private	Ⓑ
(C)	Merit	Demerit	Ⓒ
(D)	Demerit	Public	Ⓓ

7 Which of the following concepts are examples of privatisation?

(A) Regulation and nationalisation Ⓐ

(B) Deregulation and contracting out Ⓑ

(C) Franchising and redistribution Ⓒ

(D) Nationalisation and redistribution Ⓓ

8 All of the following are forms of government intervention to regulate market failure EXCEPT

(A) Anti-trust policy   Ⓐ

(B) Legislation   Ⓑ

(C) Corporate ethics   Ⓒ

(D) Lowering the age limit for smoking tobacco products   Ⓓ

1 Marginal productivity theory is used to explain how much of an input a profit maximising producer will

(A) Supply at the market price ⓐ

(B) Demand given the marginal input cost ⓑ

(C) Be prepared to hire according to the distribution of income ⓒ

(D) Be prepared to negotiate with as the input price falls ⓓ

Items **2–3** refer to the diagram below, showing different economic concepts.

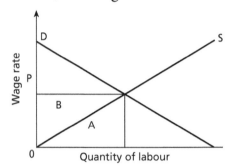

2 Which of the following economic concepts does the area of triangle A represent?

(A) Transfer earnings ⓐ

(B) Total welfare to society ⓑ

(C) Economic rent ⓒ

(D) The incidence of a tax ⓓ

3 The triangle in the diagram represented by the letter B is called

(A) Transfer earnings ⓐ

(B) Economic rent ⓑ

(C) Consumer surplus ⓒ

(D) Producer surplus ⓓ

Item **4** refers to the graph below, showing the marginal revenue product curve.

4 In the graph above, the marginal revenue product curve has shifted from MRP_1 to MRP_2.

Which of the following factors are most likely to have caused this outward shift?

(i) A rise in worker productivity

(ii) A fall in the price of the final good that labour produces

(iii) A rise in the price of the final good that labour produces

(iv) A fall in labour productivity

(A) i and iv only   Ⓐ

(B) iii and iv only   Ⓑ

(C) ii and iii only   Ⓒ

(D) i and iii only   Ⓓ

5 The MRP curve slopes downward because

(A) The marginal physical product is falling due to diminishing marginal returns to labour   Ⓐ

(B) Less labour is supplied at lower wages   Ⓑ

(C) More labour is demanded at lower wages   Ⓒ

(D) Firms seek to increase profits by reducing their wage bill   Ⓓ

<u>Item **6**</u> refers to the diagram below, showing the demand and supply for a factor of production.

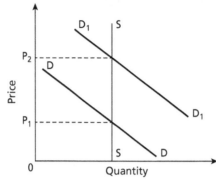

6 A shift in the demand curve from DD to D1D1 will cause

   (**A**) An increase in transfer earnings   Ⓐ

   (**B**) An increase in economic rent   Ⓑ

   (**C**) A decrease in consumer surplus   Ⓒ

   (**D**) A decrease in transfer earnings   Ⓓ

7 An outward shift in the demand curve for any product causes

   (**A**) An outward shift in the derived demand curve for one factor employed to produce the product   Ⓐ

   (**B**) An inward shift in the derived demand curve for all factors employed to produce the product   Ⓑ

   (**C**) An outward shift in the derived demand curve for all factors employed to produce the product   Ⓒ

   (**D**) An inward shift in the derived demand curve for one factor employed to produce the product   Ⓓ

8 The higher the demand for houses, and hence their prices, the higher will be the demand for masons, carpenters and plumbers. This concept best relates to

(A) Derived demand   Ⓐ

(B) Effective demand   Ⓑ

(C) Change in labour demanded   Ⓒ

(D) Change in factor demand   Ⓓ

9 As compared to a perfectly competitive labour market, a monopsonist will hire

(A) More workers earning a higher wage rate   Ⓐ

(B) Fewer workers earning a lower wage rate   Ⓑ

(C) More workers earning a lower wage rate   Ⓒ

(D) Fewer workers earning a higher wage rate   Ⓓ

10 The curve representing the supply of labour may be backward bending due to

(A) A negative income effect   Ⓐ

(B) A negative substitution effect   Ⓑ

(C) The sacrifice of leisure   Ⓒ

(D) Increased hours of work   Ⓓ

11 Transfer earnings are

(A) The transfer of pension rights when changing a job   Ⓐ

(B) The minimum payment to keep a factor of production in its current occupation   Ⓑ

(C) The increased earnings of a job promotion   Ⓒ

(D) The same as producer surplus   Ⓓ

12 A monopsonistic labour market is one in which

(A) The firm is a sole buyer of labour Ⓐ

(B) A powerful labour union is the sole supplier of labour Ⓑ

(C) The wage of the workers in this market is determined by their individual bargaining power Ⓒ

(D) Workers as a group can successfully demand higher wages Ⓓ

13 In an imperfect monopsonistic labour market, the supply curve of labour is

(A) Horizontal Ⓐ

(B) Left to right and upward sloping Ⓑ

(C) The same as the marginal wage curve Ⓒ

(D) Above the marginal wage curve Ⓓ

14 The Value of the Marginal Product of Labour (VMPL) is calculated as

(A) The marginal physical product of labour divided by the price of the product Ⓐ

(B) The average physical product of labour multiplied by the price of the product Ⓑ

(C) The marginal physical product of labour multiplied by the price of the product Ⓒ

(D) The average physical product of labour divided by the price of the product Ⓓ

15 A profit maximising monopsonist will demand labour up to where

(A) The marginal revenue product of labour is equal to the marginal wage Ⓐ

(B) The marginal revenue product of labour is equal to the average wage Ⓑ

(C) The marginal revenue product of labour is less than the marginal wage Ⓒ

(D) The marginal revenue product of labour is greater than the marginal wage Ⓓ

16 Which of the following is TRUE? A profit maximising monopsonist will demand labour up to where

(A) The marginal revenue product of labour is equal to the marginal wage and pay the average wage   Ⓐ

(B) The marginal revenue product of labour is equal to the average wage and pay the average wage   Ⓑ

(C) The marginal revenue product of labour is less than the marginal wage and pay the average wage   Ⓒ

(D) The marginal revenue product of labour is greater than the marginal wage and pay the average wage   Ⓓ

1.3.2 Wage Differentials

1 Wage differentials are BEST defined as

(A) The factors that account for differences in wage levels between workers in one industry only   Ⓐ

(B) The factors that account for differences in wage levels between workers in one industry or across many industries   Ⓑ

(C) The amount of income necessary to attain a basic standard of living   Ⓒ

(D) The income level where low income citizens pay zero taxes   Ⓓ

Item **2** refers to the diagram below which shows a monopsony buyer of labour.

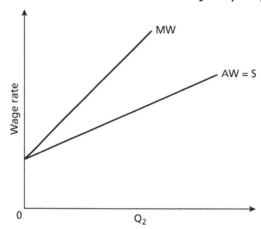

2 The marginal wage is higher than the average wage because

(A) The entire workforce has to be paid when a higher wage is offered to a new worker (A)

(B) A high wage is offered as an incentive for higher productivity (B)

(C) Powerful unions play a key role in a marginal wage negotiation (C)

(D) Governments set minimum wages which influence high marginal wages (D)

3 All of the following are factors leading to wage differentials EXCEPT

(A) The level of education and training of workers (A)

(B) The age and experience of workers (B)

(C) The demand and supply conditions of the labour market (C)

(D) A perfectly competitive labour market (D)

4 Which of the following workers is most likely to receive a compensating wage differential?

(A) A professional athlete living close to the playing stadium (A)

(B) A worker employed by the government in a grass cutting project (B)

(C) A truck driver transporting radioactive waste (C)

(D) A computer repairman (D)

5 The government may intervene in the labour market in which of the following ways?

(A) Implement closed shop supply of labour (A)

(B) Initiate industrial action (B)

(C) Enact minimum wage legislation (C)

(D) Provide financial assistance to unions (D)

6 Which of the following factors is most likely to cause a high wage to be earned?

(A) Inelastic demand for and supply of the worker's labour (A)

(B) A low price for the worker's output (B)

(C) Low productivity of the worker (C)

(D) A worker who is not a union member (D)

7 Which of the following is NOT a characteristic of a perfectly competitive labour market?

(A) All workers have the same level of skill and ability (A)

(B) All workers can have easy access to any type of employment (B)

(C) All workers have perfect knowledge of job opportunities (C)

(D) All workers have the power to command the wages they wish to earn (D)

8 In an imperfect labour market the marginal and average wage curves are

(A) Perfectly inelastic (A)

(B) Upward sloping (B)

(C) Downward sloping (C)

(D) Perfectly elastic (D)

9 In a perfectly competitive labour market the marginal revenue product is calculated as

(A) Marginal Physical Product × Average Revenue (A)

(B) Marginal Physical Product / Average Revenue (B)

(C) Total Physical Product × Marginal Revenue (C)

(D) Average Physical Product × Marginal Revenue (D)

Item 10 refers to the information given below for a perfectly competitive labour market.

	Wage rate	Quantity of Labour	
(A)	Rise	Rise	Ⓐ
(B)	Rise	Fall	Ⓑ
(C)	Fall	Fall	Ⓒ
(D)	Fall	Rise	Ⓓ

10 Which of the above (A, B, C or D) will result if a union bargains for a wage rate that is higher than the market rate?

1.3.3 Income Inequality and Poverty Alleviation

1 Which of the following is explained by the theory of income distribution?

(A) The role of government in income distribution   Ⓐ

(B) How income is distributed between different income groups   Ⓑ

(C) The role unions play in increasing wages for low wage earners   Ⓒ

(D) How wages, interest, rent and profit are allocated to factors of production   Ⓓ

2 The functional distribution of income measures the distribution of income according to

(A) Geographic location   Ⓐ

(B) The factor rewards earned by the factors of production   Ⓑ

(C) The level of incomes earned by individuals   Ⓒ

(D) The social class of individuals who earn it   Ⓓ

3 The difference between absolute and relative poverty occurs when a person

(A) Can suffer absolute poverty and satisfy their wants but is relatively poor compared to others   Ⓐ

(B) Is unable to afford a basic standard of living but is also relatively poor when living below the average income level of the country   Ⓑ

(C) Is living on the poverty line and is both absolutely and relatively poor   Ⓒ

(D) Is absolutely poor living on the line of perfect inequality and relatively poor living below the poverty line   Ⓓ

4 Which of the following countries has the greatest inequality of income distribution?

Country	Value of Gini coefficient
(A)	0.9
(B)	0.1
(C)	0.5
(D)	0.2

Ⓐ
Ⓑ
Ⓒ
Ⓓ

Items **5–6** refer to the following diagram of the Lorenz curve.

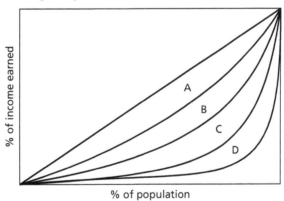

5 Which curve represents the GREATEST level of inequality?

(A) Curve D   Ⓐ

(B) Curve C   Ⓑ

(C) Curve B   Ⓒ

(D) Curve A   Ⓓ

6 Which area will have the smallest Gini coefficient?

(A) Area B   (A)

(B) Area A   (B)

(C) Area D   (C)

(D) Area C   (D)

Item 7 refers to the diagram below of a Lorenz curve

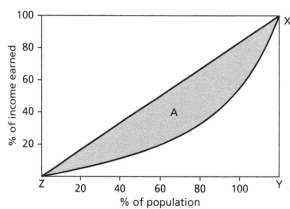

7 By expressing the shaded area A as a percentage of the triangle XYZ, an economist can calculate

(A) Income elasticity of demand   (A)

(B) The Gini coefficient   (B)

(C) Herfindahl–Hirschman index   (C)

(D) The human development index   (D)

8 The minimum level of income required to sustain life refers to

(A) The minimum poverty index   (A)

(B) The poverty line   (B)

(C) Relative poverty   (C)

(D) Absolute poverty   (D)

9 A Gini coefficient of 100% represents

(A) Total inequality of income distribution   Ⓐ

(B) Total equality of income distribution   Ⓑ

(C) Absolute poverty   Ⓒ

(D) Relative poverty   Ⓓ

10 'Longevity' is a component of which of the following measures?

(A) The Lorenz curve   Ⓐ

(B) The human development index   Ⓑ

(C) The welfare index   Ⓒ

(D) The standard of living index   Ⓓ

11 The following are different measures of poverty EXCEPT

(A) The Gini coefficient   Ⓐ

(B) The poverty line   Ⓑ

(C) Basic needs measure   Ⓒ

(D) The headcount index   Ⓓ

Unit 2:
Macroeconomics

Module 1: Models of the Macroeconomy
2.1.1 National Income Accounting

1 Which of the following best defines real national income? Note that GDP = Gross Domestic Product and GNP = Gross National Product as it relates to questions in Module 1.

(A) Nominal GDP in any year   (A)

(B) National income adjusted for the rise in the average price level   (B)

(C) GDP plus net property going abroad   (C)

(D) GNP minus depreciation   (D)

2 Which of the following BEST defines GDP?

(A) The total market value of output produced in a country measured annually   (A)

(B) The total market value of output produced in a country including the value of imports   (B)

(C) The total market value of output produced in a country adjusted for net property income   (C)

(D) The total market value of output produced in a country adjusted for depreciation   (D)

3 GDP at market prices minus indirect taxes and plus subsidies is equal to

(A) GDP at constant costs   (A)

(B) GDP at factor costs   (B)

(C) GNP at current prices   (C)

(D) Nominal GDP   (D)

4 In country A, the year 2016 is used as the base year for measuring real GDP. What is the value of the price index in the year 2016?

(A) 100   (A)

(B) 1   (B)

(C) 200   (C)

(D) 0   (D)

Items **5–6** refer to the following table.

Item	$m
Exports and net property income from abroad	120
Imports and net property income paid abroad	80
Indirect taxes	40
Subsidies	20
Total domestic expenditure at market prices	300

5 What is the gross national product at factor cost?

(A) $560

(B) $320

(C) $280

(D) $360

    Ⓐ

    Ⓑ

    Ⓒ

    Ⓓ

6 What is the gross national product at market prices?

(A) $560

(B) $340

(C) $400

(D) $360

    Ⓐ

    Ⓑ

    Ⓒ

    Ⓓ

Items **7–8** refer to the following information.

Country A produces two goods: Good X and Good Y. The information below shows the quantities produced and the prices in 2015 and 2016.

	2015		2016	
Goods	**Quantity**	**Price ($)**	**Quantity**	**Price ($)**
A	10	5	20	8
B	50	3	40	6

7 Nominal GDP in 2016 was

(A) $160   (A)

(B) $240   (B)

(C) $400   (C)

(D) $180   (D)

8 Real GDP in 2016 was

(A) $180   (A)

(B) $160   (B)

(C) $400   (C)

(D) $220   (D)

9 In GDP calculations, the value of intermediate goods is

(A) Counted at market prices   (A)

(B) Not counted   (B)

(C) Counted in addition to the final value   (C)

(D) Counted but adjusted for subsidies received from the government   (D)

10 Which of the following items is NOT counted in GDP calculations?

(A) The price of a haircut   (A)

(B) Newly purchased equipment   (B)

(C) A salesman's commission on a used car   (C)

(D) The sale of used goods   (D)

1 Classical theorists believed that the underlying reason for long-term unemployment was

(A) Demand deficient   (A)

(B) Determined by a recession   (B)

(C) Technology replacing labour   (C)

(D) People individually deciding not to work   (D)

Item 2 refers to the diagram below, which shows two aggregate supply curves of an economy.

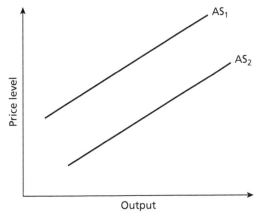

2 Which of the following expressions is most likely to be the reason that the AS_1 curve has shifted to AS_2?

(A) An increase in the cost of variable factors   (A)

(B) A withdrawal of cost-of-living allowances from those employed   (B)

(C) An increase in labour productivity   (C)

(D) Replacing technology with manual labour   (D)

3 The slope of the classical aggregate supply curve is

(A) At first elastic then inelastic in the short run   (A)

(B) At first inelastic then elastic in the long run   (B)

(C) Upward sloping throughout   (C)

(D) Perfectly elastic in the long run

4 Classical theorists believe that the employment of supply side economic measures will

(A) Increase the price level and reduce real domestic output   Ⓐ

(B) Reduce the level of inflation and increase real domestic output   Ⓑ

(C) Reduce the price level and real domestic output   Ⓒ

(D) Have no effect on the price level or real domestic output   Ⓓ

5 'Supply creates its own demand'. This statement is the view of

(A) Keynesian theorists   Ⓐ

(B) Monetarist theorists   Ⓑ

(C) Classical theorist J.B. Say   Ⓒ

(D) Rationalist theorists   Ⓓ

6 Classical theorists held the view that this capital market will always be in equilibrium because

(A) Interest rates are flexible and would be responsive to market forces in the capital market   Ⓐ

(B) The central bank would intervene in the event of surpluses or shortages of capital   Ⓑ

(C) There is always excess liquidity in the financial system   Ⓒ

(D) The market will be effectively managed by the government   Ⓓ

7 Which of the following is a concept of monetarist theorists?

(A) The multiplier   Ⓐ

(B) The quantity theory   Ⓑ

(C) Aggregate demand creates aggregate supply   Ⓒ

(D) The use of fiscal policy as the main tool of economic management   Ⓓ

8 Classical theorists claim that interest rates are a deciding factor in maintaining capital market equilibrium. Which of the following are reasons advanced against this claim?

    (I) Keynes' claim that business expectations have a bigger influence on investment than the rate of interest

   (II) Say's law of markets is valid

  (III) Disequilibrium will persist in all markets and will not clear automatically

  (IV) The quantity theory is valid

(A) I and II only   Ⓐ

(B) II and IV only   Ⓑ

(C) I and III only   Ⓒ

(D) I and IV only   Ⓓ

9 The long run aggregate supply curve is

(A) Perfectly elastic   Ⓐ

(B) Inelastic   Ⓑ

(C) Horizontal   Ⓒ

(D) Perfectly inelastic   Ⓓ

2.1.3 Keynesian Models of the Economy

1 Keynesian economics emphasise a key role in the economy for

(A) Free market forces   Ⓐ

(B) Supply side management   Ⓑ

(C) Fiscal policy   Ⓒ

(D) Monetary policy   Ⓓ

<u>Items **2–3**</u> refer to the diagram of the consumption function.

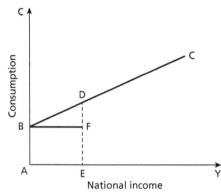

2 In the diagram, AB represents

    (A) Induced consumption   Ⓐ

    (B) Autonomous consumption   Ⓑ

    (C) Variable consumption   Ⓒ

    (D) The marginal propensity to consume   Ⓓ

3 In the diagram, the marginal propensity to consume is represented by which of the following expressions?

    (A) AB / AE   Ⓐ

    (B) BF / DE   Ⓑ

    (C) DE / AE   Ⓒ

    (D) DF / BF   Ⓓ

Item **4** refers to the diagram below of a consumption function YC_1.

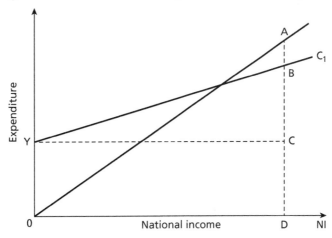

4 What does BD / AD represent?

(A) The average propensity to consume   Ⓐ

(B) Induced consumption   Ⓑ

(C) Consumption minus expenditure   Ⓒ

(D) Autonomous consumption   Ⓓ

Item **5** refers to the information below, showing the values for consumption at different levels of income.

Income ($)	Consumption
0	60
100	140
200	220
300	300
400	380

5 Which of the following equations represents the consumption function from the information given above?

(A) $C = 60 + 0.8Y_d$ Ⓐ

(B) $C = 100 + 140Y_d$ Ⓑ

(C) $C = 80 + 100Y$ Ⓒ

(D) $C = 60 / 0.8Y_d$ Ⓓ

Item **6** refers to the following diagram, which shows a savings function.

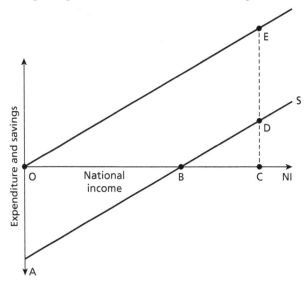

6 Which of the following expressions represents the marginal propensity to save?

(A) DC / BC   Ⓐ

(B) ED / CD   Ⓑ

(C) DE / BC   Ⓒ

(D) DC / OC   Ⓓ

7 The MAJOR difference between induced consumption and autonomous consumption is that induced consumption is influenced by changes in

(A) The state of the economy   Ⓐ

(B) The rate of inflation   Ⓑ

(C) The rate of taxation   Ⓒ

(D) Disposable income   Ⓓ

Items **8–9** refer to the diagrams below which show the equilibrium national income Y and the full employment level Y_F. AE = Aggregate expenditure; NI = National income.

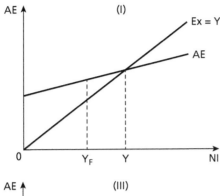
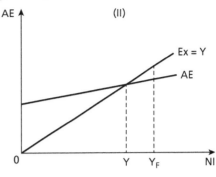
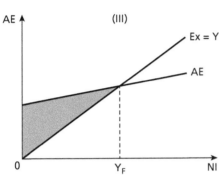
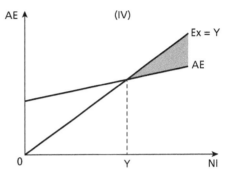

8 Which of the diagrams represents a recessionary gap?

(A) I (A)

(B) II (B)

(C) III (C)

(D) IV (D)

9 Which of the diagrams represents an inflationary gap?

(A) I (A)

(B) II (B)

(C) III (C)

(D) IV (D)

Item **10** refers to the following diagram showing dissavings.

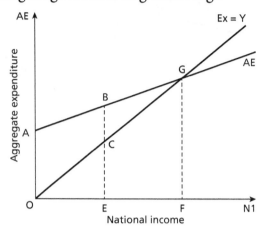

10 Which of the following segments BEST represents dissavings?

    (A) BC   Ⓐ

    (B) OCBA   Ⓑ

    (C) OCGBA   Ⓒ

    (D) CBG   Ⓓ

Item **11** refers to the following diagram of the savings function in millions of dollars.

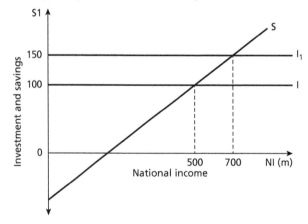

11 The diagram shows that national income has increased from $500 million to $700 million. All values are expressed in millions. What is the marginal propensity to consume?

(A) 75   Ⓐ

(B) 25   Ⓑ

(C) 1   Ⓒ

(D) 8   Ⓓ

12 The relationship between the marginal propensity to consume and the average propensity to consume is

(A) Both rise and fall at the same rate   Ⓐ

(B) While the average propensity to consume is constant, the marginal propensity to consume is falling   Ⓑ

(C) While the marginal propensity to consume is constant, the average propensity to consume is falling   Ⓒ

(D) Both rise and fall at different rates   Ⓓ

Items **13–15** refer to the information below expressed in millions of dollars:

Consumption = 40 + 0.5Y; Investment = 60; Government Spending = 200; Net Exports (NX) = 100.

13 Given the information above, what is the equilibrium level of national income?

(A) $400   Ⓐ

(B) $800   Ⓑ

(C) $10 000   Ⓒ

(D) $3600   Ⓓ

14 From the information given, the value of the multiplier is

(A) 1.4   Ⓐ

(B) 2.5   Ⓑ

(C) 2   Ⓒ

(D) 6   Ⓓ

15 The national income equilibrium is $20 billion but the full employment level of national income is $30 billion. If the consumption function is given as $C = 40 + 0.6Y$, by how much should government spending increase in order to achieve the full employment level of national income?

(A) $400 billion   (A)

(B) $500 billion   (B)

(C) $250 billion   (C)

(D) $600 billion   (D)

2.1.4 Investment

1 Unplanned investment takes place when

(A) Aggregate supply is greater than aggregate demand   (A)

(B) Aggregate demand is greater than aggregate supply   (B)

(C) The economy is experiencing an inflationary gap   (C)

(D) The economy is in national income equilibrium   (D)

2 Unplanned disinvestment takes place when

(A) There are reductions from stock when aggregate demand is greater than aggregate supply   (A)

(B) Aggregate supply is greater than aggregate demand   (B)

(C) There is an overproduction of goods and services by firms in a given year   (C)

(D) There are additions to stock caused by a fall in aggregate demand   (D)

3 The relationship between the rate and magnitude of changes in national output and changes in investment is explained by which of the following concepts?

(A) The multiplier Ⓐ

(B) The marginal efficiency of capital Ⓑ

(C) The accelerator principle Ⓒ

(D) The marginal efficiency of investment Ⓓ

4 The relationship between the marginal efficiency of investment and the rate of interest may be described as

(A) Inverse Ⓐ

(B) Positive Ⓑ

(C) Complementary Ⓒ

(D) Neutral Ⓓ

5 All of the following factors may cause an outward shift in the marginal efficiency of investment EXCEPT

(A) The introduction of new technology Ⓐ

(B) An increase in the productivity of capital Ⓑ

(C) A decrease in the rate of interest Ⓒ

(D) An increase in the price of the output that capital produces Ⓓ

6 All of the following are limitations of the accelerator principle EXCEPT

(A) The theory assumes that firms do not have spare capacity Ⓐ

(B) The supply of capital in the short term may be inelastic Ⓑ

(C) Firms may introduce more production shifts instead of purchasing new capital Ⓒ

(D) There are no time lags between changes in national output and changes in investment Ⓓ

7 All of the following factors cause investment to be volatile EXCEPT

(A) The durability of capital   Ⓐ

(B) The rate of innovation   Ⓑ

(C) Variability of profit   Ⓒ

(D) Constant capital output ratios   Ⓓ

8 The accelerator principle may be represented by which of the following expressions?

(A) $1 / 1 - b$ Ⓐ

(B) $I_N = a$ (change in NI) where I_n is investment, a is the capital output ratio and NI is national income   Ⓑ

(C) $I_N =$ change in national income   Ⓒ

(D) Investment / Total income   Ⓓ

9 The marginal efficiency of a capital curve is

(A) The supply curve for capital   Ⓐ

(B) The demand curve for capital   Ⓑ

(C) Upward sloping   Ⓒ

(D) Perfectly inelastic   Ⓓ

10 The MEC curve is downward sloping due to

(A) Increasing estimated future returns to capital   Ⓐ

(B) Diminishing estimated future returns to capital   Ⓑ

(C) Falling interest rates   Ⓒ

(D) Constant estimated returns to capital   Ⓓ

1 Unemployment is BEST associated with which of the following concepts?

(A) An inflationary gap Ⓐ

(B) A deflationary gap Ⓑ

(C) Economic growth Ⓒ

(D) A budget surplus Ⓓ

2 The relationship between unemployment and inflation is reflected in which of the following curves?

(A) The aggregate supply of labour curve Ⓐ

(B) The aggregate demand of labour curve Ⓑ

(C) The Phillips curve Ⓒ

(D) The labour participation curve Ⓓ

3 The relationship between unemployment and inflation, according to the Phillips curve, is that as inflation rises unemployment

(A) Falls Ⓐ

(B) Rises Ⓑ

(C) Remains constant Ⓒ

(D) Remains unchanged Ⓓ

4 The aggregate supply of labour curve shows

(A) The total amount of factor inputs supplied Ⓐ

(B) The average number of people who are willing to work Ⓑ

(C) The total number of people who are willing to work at different wage rates Ⓒ

(D) The average number of people who are willing to work at different wage rates Ⓓ

5 Which of the following groups of persons are counted in the labour force participation rate?

(A) Full-time students at tertiary level of studies   Ⓐ

(B) Full-time housewives   Ⓑ

(C) Persons already employed or actively looking for employment   Ⓒ

(D) Totally disabled people   Ⓓ

Item **6** refers to the graph below, which shows the classical model for a labour market.

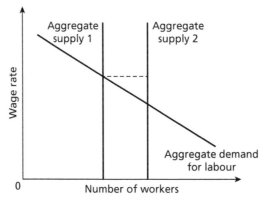

6 The dotted line indicates

(A) Unemployed labour   Ⓐ

(B) A shortage of labour   Ⓑ

(C) The natural rate of unemployment   Ⓒ

(D) The unemployed who are willing to work   Ⓓ

7 According to the Keynesian model, the main reason for high levels of unemployment is

(A) A lack of aggregate demand   Ⓐ

(B) A lack of aggregate supply   Ⓑ

(C) A budget deficit   Ⓒ

(D) An increase in the average price level   Ⓓ

8 Classical theorists held the view that labour market unemployment was voluntary because

(A) People prefer to invest their money for a return rather than work ⒶA

(B) Any disequilibrium in the labour market will be corrected by market forces since the wage rate is flexible, so anyone who is unemployed chooses to remain so ⒷB

(C) Any shortfall in employment opportunities will be provided by the government through special projects ⒸC

(D) Occupational and geographic mobility enables anyone to find a job when they need one ⒹD

9 Under the Caribbean Single Market and Economy (CSME) agreement, an engineer from Jamaica now works as a hotelier in St. Lucia. What types of labour mobility have taken place?

(I) Horizontal

(II) Occupational

(III) Geographical

(IV) Vertical

(A) I and III only ⒶA

(B) II and IV only ⒷB

(C) II and III only ⒸC

(D) III and IV only ⒹD

10 The labour force participation rate can BEST be described as the ratio of

(A) The population to the labour force ⒶA

(B) The employed to the population ⒷB

(C) The employed to the unemployed ⒸC

(D) The labour force to the population ⒹD

11 The term 'price index' is BEST explained as

(A) A persistent increase in the price level over time   Ⓐ

(B) A measurement indicating how the average price of a basket of goods changes over time   Ⓑ

(C) A numerical value given to an average basket of goods   Ⓒ

(D) A measurement of the changes in base year prices   Ⓓ

12 The statement 'too much money chasing too few goods' refers to

(A) Cost push inflation   Ⓐ

(B) Cost pull inflation   Ⓑ

(C) Demand push inflation   Ⓒ

(D) Demand pull inflation   Ⓓ

13 All of the following measures can be used to measure inflation EXCEPT

(A) The retail price index   Ⓐ

(B) The income method   Ⓑ

(C) The producer price index   Ⓒ

(D) The tax and price index   Ⓓ

14 Given the following data:

Money supply (M) = 200

Number of transactions (T) = 400

Velocity of circulation (V) = 5

If the price level rises by 25%, then by how much would the money supply increase?

(A) 50%   Ⓐ

(B) 75%   Ⓑ

(C) 25%   Ⓒ

(D) 100%   Ⓓ

15 The velocity of circulation can be defined as

(A) The number of times in a given time period that a unit of currency is used to purchase the final output of a country Ⓐ

(B) The total number of transactions divided by the average price level Ⓑ

(C) The average price level multiplied by the total number of transactions Ⓒ

(D) The money supply in a given time period divided by the average price level Ⓓ

16 If the rate of inflation in the base year 2015 was 100 and subsequently 110 in 2016, then the rate of inflation

(A) Fell by 10% Ⓐ

(B) Rose by 10% Ⓑ

(C) Rose by 210% Ⓒ

(D) Fell by 210% Ⓓ

17 All of the following factors can contribute to cost push inflation except

(A) An increase in the exchange rate Ⓐ

(B) A rise in wage levels Ⓑ

(C) A rise in indirect taxes Ⓒ

(D) A fall in interest rates Ⓓ

18 A high rate of inflation can over time cause

(A) A balance of trade deficit Ⓐ

(B) An increase in the commodity terms of trade Ⓑ

(C) A balance of payments surplus Ⓒ

(D) Government spending to rise Ⓓ

19 Which of the following is NOT an example of a redistributive effect caused by inflation?

(A) Borrowers gain at the expense of lenders   (A)

(B) Foreign firms gain at the expense of domestic firms   (B)

(C) Weak labour unions gain from the actions of strong labour unions   (C)

(D) Taxpayers gain at the expense of the government   (D)

20 When aggregate demand exceeds aggregate supply at the full employment level of output, this leads to

(A) Cost push inflation   (A)

(B) Demand pull inflation   (B)

(C) Fiscal imbalance   (C)

(D) Negative growth   (D)

2.2.2 Monetary Theory and Policy

1 Which of the following two factors BEST determine the demand for money?

(I) The level of investment

(II) The level of income

(III) The rate of interest

(IV) The market prices of goods

(A) I and IV only   (A)

(B) II and III only   (B)

(C) I and II only   (C)

(D) III and IV only   (D)

2 The precautionary demand for holding money is determined by

(A) The price of securities falling Ⓐ

(B) The period between paydays Ⓑ

(C) Speculation on bond prices Ⓒ

(D) A lack of reliable information on receipts and revenue inflows Ⓓ

3 The central bank has the sole authority for the quantity of money supplied. The money supply curve is therefore

(A) Downward sloping Ⓐ

(B) Perfectly elastic in supply Ⓑ

(C) Perfectly inelastic in supply Ⓒ

(D) Positively sloped Ⓓ

4 Which of the following central bank's actions is considered to be an example of expansionary monetary policy?

(A) An increase in the cash reserve ratio Ⓐ

(B) A decrease in open market purchases of commercial banks' securities Ⓑ

(C) A decrease in the overnight lending (repo) rate Ⓒ

(D) An increase in special deposits Ⓓ

5 The speculative demand for holding money is determined by the function of money as a

(A) Store of value Ⓐ

(B) Standard for deferred payment Ⓑ

(C) Measure of value Ⓒ

(D) Medium of exchange Ⓓ

<u>Item **6**</u> refers to the diagrams below which show the demand for (downward sloping LP curve) and supply of money. Note that MS1 = Money supply 1; LP = Liquidity preference; Qm = quantity of money.

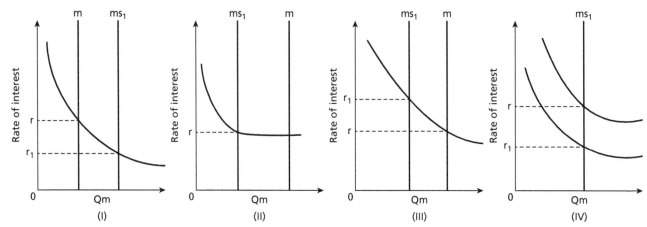

6 Which diagram shows monetary policy aimed at reducing the rate of demand inflation?

(A) I   Ⓐ

(B) II   Ⓑ

(C) III   Ⓒ

(D) IV   Ⓓ

7 One of the limitations of monetary policy is that

(A) It is difficult to reverse   Ⓐ

(B) It is counteracted by expansionary fiscal policy   Ⓑ

(C) It can lead to policy conflict   Ⓒ

(D) The overnight lending rate works too quickly   Ⓓ

8 Which of the following measures of the money supply represents cash in circulation and cheque account deposits only?

(A) M_0

(B) M_1

(C) $M_0 + M_1$

(D) M_2

Ⓐ
Ⓑ
Ⓒ
Ⓓ

9 The government sells treasury bills using open market operations. The effect of this action on the rate of interest and the money supply is

	Interest rate	Money supply
(A)	Rises	Falls
(B)	Falls	Rises
(C)	Rises	Rises
(D)	Falls	Falls

Ⓐ
Ⓑ
Ⓒ
Ⓓ

10 An outward shift of the liquidity preference schedule can be caused by

(A) A fall in the interest rate

(B) Speculation of a rise in bond prices

(C) An increase in national income

(D) A recession

Ⓐ
Ⓑ
Ⓒ
Ⓓ

2.2.3 Fiscal Policy

1 Which of the following is an example of contractionary fiscal policy?

(A) An increase in the interest rate Ⓐ

(B) An increase in direct taxation Ⓑ

(C) An increase in government spending Ⓒ

(D) An increase in the national debt Ⓓ

<u>Item 2</u> refers to the diagram below, showing government spending and tax revenue.

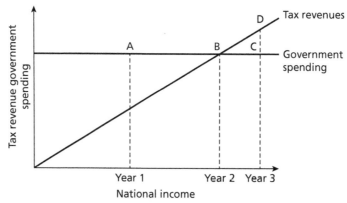

2 What type of policy is being pursued by the government at point A?

(A) Budget deficit Ⓐ

(B) Balanced budget Ⓑ

(C) Exchange rate policy Ⓒ

(D) Interest rate policy Ⓓ

3 Examples of automatic stabilisers are

    (I) Unemployment benefits

    (II) Indirect taxes

    (III) A rise in interest rates

    (IV) Farm price supports

(A) I and IV only   Ⓐ

(B) II and III only   Ⓑ

(C) I and III only   Ⓒ

(D) I and II only   Ⓓ

4 One of the roles of automatic stabilisers is to

    (I) Increase economic growth

    (II) Reverse a recession

    (III) Cushion the economy from the onset of a recession

    (IV) Insulate the economy from internal shocks

(A) I and II only   Ⓐ

(B) II and IV only   Ⓑ

(C) I and IV only   Ⓒ

(D) III and IV only   Ⓓ

5 Which of the following fiscal measures should a government take in a recession?

(A) A budget surplus   Ⓐ

(B) A budget deficit   Ⓑ

(C) A balanced budget   Ⓒ

(D) An increase in the rate of interest   Ⓓ

6 A budget surplus can be employed to

(A) Remove an inflationary gap   Ⓐ

(B) Increase aggregate demand   Ⓑ

(C) Increase import spending   Ⓒ

(D) Increase economic growth   Ⓓ

7 The balanced budget multiplier is equal to

(A) 10   Ⓐ

(B) 5   Ⓑ

(C) 1   Ⓒ

(D) 0.75   Ⓓ

8 The delay that takes place before a fiscal measure achieves the planned outcome is called

(A) The fiscal delay   Ⓐ

(B) The time deficit   Ⓑ

(C) Fiscal lag   Ⓒ

(D) Fiscal indiscipline   Ⓓ

9 All of the following are limitations of fiscal policy EXCEPT

(A) Policy conflict   Ⓐ

(B) Resource crowding out   Ⓑ

(C) It can achieve all policy objectives at the same time   Ⓒ

(D) Government expenditure is difficult to reduce   Ⓓ

10 The Laffer curve indicates that the incentive effect of lowering income tax rates would

(A) Increase tax revenue   Ⓐ

(B) Decrease tax revenue   Ⓑ

(C) Cause the rate of unemployment to rise   Ⓒ

(D) Cause the rate of inflation to rise   Ⓓ

11 Which of the following fiscal measures is MOST likely to reduce the rate of demand pull inflation?

(A) A budget surplus   Ⓐ

(B) A budget deficit   Ⓑ

(C) A reduction in income taxes   Ⓒ

(D) An increase in indirect taxation   Ⓓ

2.2.4 The Public Debt

1 All of the following are sources used by the government to finance the national debt EXCEPT

(A) The banking sector   Ⓐ

(B) The non-banking sector   Ⓑ

(C) Foreign creditors   Ⓒ

(D) The International Monetary Fund   Ⓓ

2 Which of the following is not an effect of government borrowing on the economy in the short term?

(A) Financial crowding out   Ⓐ

(B) Diversion of financial resources to external creditors   Ⓑ

(C) A fall in the average price level   Ⓒ

(D) An increase in the interest rate   Ⓓ

3 Which of the following can BEST result in a reduction of the national debt?

(A) A budget deficit   Ⓐ

(B) A budget surplus   Ⓑ

(C) A recession   Ⓒ

(D) A deflationary gap   Ⓓ

4 The debt ratio is represented by which of the following expressions?

(A) Principal + interest / Export earnings   Ⓐ

(B) Principal + interest / The national debt   Ⓑ

(C) GDP / Principal + interest   Ⓒ

(D) Principal + interest / GDP   Ⓓ

5 The debt service ratio is represented by which of the following?

(A) Principal + interest / Export earnings   Ⓐ

(B) Principal + interest / The national debt   Ⓑ

(C) Interest payable / Export earnings   Ⓒ

(D) Principal + interest / GDP   Ⓓ

6 The national debt may be defined as

(A) The total sum borrowed for one year   Ⓐ

(B) The total accumulated debt of past years   Ⓑ

(C) Principal + interest / Export earnings   Ⓒ

(D) Principal + interest / GDP   Ⓓ

7 Which of the following will cause the national debt to be a burden?

(A) The debt is owed to foreigners   Ⓐ

(B) The debt can be exchanged for equity   Ⓑ

(C) The debt is transferred from one generation to the next   Ⓒ

(D) The debt can be refinanced   Ⓓ

8 All of the following can be used to manage a high public debt EXCEPT

(A) Debt rescheduling   Ⓐ

(B) Debt forgiveness   Ⓑ

(C) Debt retirement   Ⓒ

(D) Debt default   Ⓓ

9 A debt trap is defined as

(A) Under 50% debt to GDP ratio   Ⓐ

(B) Under 100% debt to GDP ratio   Ⓑ

(C) Over 200% debt to GDP ratio   Ⓒ

(D) Between 100% and 120% debt to GDP ratio   Ⓓ

<u>Item 1</u> refers to the production possibility frontier of country X in the diagram below.

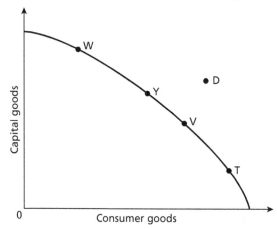

1 An outward shift of the PPF to point D can MOST likely be achieved by country X producing at which of the following points?

(A) T   (A)

(B) V   (B)

(C) W   (C)

(D) Y   (D)

2 Which of the following BEST defines economic growth?

(A) An increase in quantity of new resources discovered over time   (A)

(B) An increase in real per capita output over time   (B)

(C) A shift of the production possibility frontier inward   (C)

(D) An increase in life expectancy and literacy levels   (D)

3 To which of the following concepts do 'enlargement of choices, sustainability and equity' BEST apply?

(A) Economic growth   Ⓐ

(B) Economic development   Ⓑ

(C) Globalisation   Ⓒ

(D) Trade liberalisation   Ⓓ

4 Sustainable development can be BEST achieved for a country if

(A) All available resources are employed and production distributed equitably   Ⓐ

(B) A country can achieve sustainable growth rates exceeding 8%   Ⓑ

(C) There is an equitable distribution of income in the country   Ⓒ

(D) Human development can be sustained without depleting the existing stock of resources   Ⓓ

5 All of the following are structural characteristics of Caribbean economies EXCEPT

(A) Small sized open economies   Ⓐ

(B) Low dependence on foreign investment   Ⓑ

(C) Poorly diversified economies   Ⓒ

(D) Low productivity levels   Ⓓ

6 The characteristics of Caribbean economies place them at a disadvantage with respect to

(I) Dependence on aid

(II) Change in world prices for primary products

(III) Internal and external shocks

(IV) Preferential trade agreements

(A) I and IV only   Ⓐ

(B) II and III only   Ⓑ

(C) I, II and III only   Ⓒ

(D) All of the above   Ⓓ

Items **7–8** refer to the information below on the human development index.

Country	HDI
W	0.07
X	0.87
Y	0.55
Z	0.09

7 Which country would have the lowest level of human development?

(A) W   Ⓐ

(B) Y   Ⓑ

(C) X   Ⓒ

(D) Z   Ⓓ

8 Which country would have the highest level of human development?

(A) W   Ⓐ

(B) Y   Ⓑ

(C) X   Ⓒ

(D) Z   Ⓓ

9 If a country had an inflation rate of 10% while the rate of nominal GDP growth was 5%, this would result in

(A) Negative real economic growth   Ⓐ

(B) Negative nominal growth   Ⓑ

(C) Positive real economic growth   Ⓒ

(D) Negative economic growth   Ⓓ

10 All of the following are measures of human development EXCEPT

(A) The Human Development Index   Ⓐ

(B) The Physical Quality of Life Index   Ⓑ

(C) The Measure of Economic Welfare   Ⓒ

(D) The Gini coefficient   Ⓓ

2.3.2 International Trade

1 Which of the following are factors which determine export revenue?

  (I) International prices

 (II) Domestic production

(III) Import tariffs

(IV) Exchange rates

(A) II, III and IV only   Ⓐ

(B) I, II and IV only   Ⓑ

(C) I, III and IV only   Ⓒ

(D) I, II and III only   Ⓓ

2 Which of the following underlines the importance of export revenue to Caribbean countries?

  (I) Access to capital goods

 (II) Export generated growth

(III) Access to consumer goods

(IV) Increased domestic production

(A) I, II and III only   Ⓐ

(B) II, III and IV only   Ⓑ

(C) I, III and IV only   Ⓒ

(D) All of the above   Ⓓ

3 Both Grenada and St. Vincent produce bananas and citrus. Grenada is said to have a comparative advantage in bananas when

(A) The opportunity cost of producing bananas is greater than St. Vincent   Ⓐ

(B) It can produce both bananas and citrus with double the input factors required by St. Vincent   Ⓑ

(C) Units of bananas exchange for the same units of citrus in Grenada   Ⓒ

(D) The amount of bananas given up per unit of citrus produced is less than St. Vincent   Ⓓ

Item **4** refers to the information given below.

The table below refers to the production of fruits and vegetables in Guyana and Jamaica, both using the same units of land and labour.

	Fruits (kg)	Vegetables (kg)
Guyana	150	300
Jamaica	50	150

4 From the information above, it is correct to state that

  (I) Guyana has an absolute advantage in vegetables

  (II) Jamaica has a comparative advantage in vegetables only

  (III) Both countries can gain from trade according to absolute advantage

  (IV) Guyana has a comparative advantage in fruits

(A) I, II and IV only   Ⓐ

(B) I and III only   Ⓑ

(C) II and III only   Ⓒ

(D) I and II only   Ⓓ

5 What effect/effects will a tariff have on the quantity of apples imported by Antigua from the United States?

(A) The volume of apples traded will remain the same   Ⓐ

(B) The price of apples in Antigua will increase and the price in the United States will fall   Ⓑ

(C) The price of apples in Antigua will fall and the price in the United States will rise   Ⓒ

(D) The volume of apples traded will rise   Ⓓ

6 All of the following are reasons advanced for protectionist measures EXCEPT

(A) To protect infant industries in the importing country   Ⓐ

(B) To resolve a balance of payments deficit in the importing country   Ⓑ

(C) To protect employment in the importing country   Ⓒ

(D) To resolve a balance of trade surplus in the importing country   Ⓓ

7 Developing countries may try to boost their levels of exports by

(A) Imposing protectionist measures against imports   Ⓐ

(B) Allowing the rate of inflation to increase   Ⓑ

(C) Increasing productivity overall   Ⓒ

(D) Exiting free trade areas   Ⓓ

8 Which of the following expressions represents the commodity terms of trade?

(A) Index of export prices / Index of import prices $\times$ 100   Ⓐ

(B) Index of import prices / Index of export prices $\times$ 100   Ⓑ

(C) Export prices – Import prices   Ⓒ

(D) Import prices – Export prices   Ⓓ

9 All of the following can cause the terms of trade to be favourable EXCEPT

(A) Export prices rising faster than import prices (A)

(B) Import prices rising faster than export prices (B)

(C) Import prices remain unchanged while export prices are rising (C)

(D) Import prices are falling faster than export prices (D)

10 An increase in export revenue can MOST likely cause an increase in which of the following?

(A) Interest rates (A)

(B) The national debt (B)

(C) The money supply (C)

(D) Foreign exchange controls (D)

2.3.3 Balance of Payments and Exchange Rates

1 A systemic record of the financial flows between a country and the rest of the world is called

(A) The merchandise account (A)

(B) The balance of trade (B)

(C) The balance of payments account (C)

(D) The financial account (D)

2 Transactions recorded in the balance of payments are interpreted as

(A) Net liabilities   (A)

(B) Balance sheet items   (B)

(C) Assets   (C)

(D) Flows   (D)

3 Which of the following will be MOST likely to decrease when exchange controls are employed to rectify a balance of payments deficit?

(A) The level of imports   (A)

(B) The level of exports   (B)

(C) Interest rates   (C)

(D) The rate of inflation   (D)

Item **4** refers to the balance of payments of country X.

Current account	$ billions
Exports	150
Imports	100
Transfers inward	+50
Transfers outward	+25
Investment and other capital flows	+200

4 The current account balance of country X is

(A) $25 billion   (A)

(B) $100 billion   (B)

(C) $75 billion   (C)

(D) $100 billion   (D)

5 Which of the following measures would be MOST likely to resolve a balance of payments deficit?

(A) An expansionary monetary policy   Ⓐ

(B) An expansionary fiscal policy   Ⓑ

(C) The removal of protectionist measures   Ⓒ

(D) The implementation of foreign exchange controls   Ⓓ

6 Which of the following is MOST likely to cause a balance of payments surplus?

(A) An increase in the domestic rate of inflation compared to other countries   Ⓐ

(B) A global recession   Ⓑ

(C) A low rate of domestic inflation compared to other countries   Ⓒ

(D) A steady increase in the external value of the currency of the exporting country   Ⓓ

7 Which of the following is an expenditure-switching measure designed to rectify a balance of payments deficit?

    (I) An import quota

    (II) An expansionary monetary policy

    (III) Contractionary fiscal policy

    (IV) A tariff

(A) II and IV only   Ⓐ

(B) I and IV only   Ⓑ

(C) I and III only   Ⓒ

(D) II and III only   Ⓓ

8 Which of the following can be considered an expenditure-reducing method that can be implemented to rectify a balance of payments deficit?

(A) A budget deficit   Ⓐ

(B) An increase in interest rates   Ⓑ

(C) An import quota   Ⓒ

(D) Import substitution   Ⓓ

9 A fixed exchange rate is determined by

(A) Free market forces   Ⓐ

(B) The international monetary fund   Ⓑ

(C) The central bank of a country on behalf of the government   Ⓒ

(D) Allowing the rate to vary in a range between a high fixed rate and a low fixed rate   Ⓓ

10 An advantage of a flexible exchange rate is that it

(I) Causes the balance of payments to automatically balance if there is a deficit or surplus

(II) Discourages speculation of a currency

(III) Requires the intervention of the central bank

(IV) Is responsive to the domestic rate of inflation

(A) I and II   Ⓐ

(B) I and IV   Ⓑ

(C) II and IV   Ⓒ

(D) III and IV   Ⓓ

11 An advantage of a fixed exchange rate is that it

(A) Requires the government to keep track of its value on a daily basis   Ⓐ

(B) Allows the balance of payments to balance automatically   Ⓑ

(C) Requires the intervention of the government to support the exchange rate   Ⓒ

(D) Encourages speculation of a currency   Ⓓ

12 The appreciation of a country's currency can

(A) Be likely to lead to a balance of payments surplus Ⓐ

(B) Cause exports to become more expensive Ⓑ

(C) Cause imports to become cheaper Ⓒ

(D) Cause a balance of trade surplus Ⓓ

13 The depreciation of a country's currency can have a

(A) Likely negative effect on the balance of payments Ⓐ

(B) Likely positive effect on the level of exports Ⓑ

(C) Likely positive effect on the level of imports Ⓒ

(D) Likely negative effect on the balance of trade Ⓓ

14 If the external value of a country's currency steadily falls relative to other currencies, this is called

(A) A devaluation Ⓐ

(B) A depreciation Ⓑ

(C) Relative devaluation Ⓒ

(D) Appreciation Ⓓ

1 Which of the following BEST defines a customs union?

(A) There is free movement of factors of production between member countries   Ⓐ

(B) There are no trade barriers between members but a common external tariff to non-members   Ⓑ

(C) There are no trade barriers between member countries but there are different rates of tariff to non-members   Ⓒ

(D) All member countries have a common monetary unit and harmonised economic policy   Ⓓ

2 All of the following are examples of non-tariff barriers EXCEPT

(A) Quotas   Ⓐ

(B) Import taxes on luxury goods   Ⓑ

(C) Foreign exchange controls   Ⓒ

(D) Embargoes   Ⓓ

3 When a country becomes a member of a customs union and shifts from trading with a low price producer to a high price producer, this results in

(A) Trade diversion   Ⓐ

(B) Trade creation   Ⓑ

(C) Trade deficit   Ⓒ

(D) Balance of payments surplus   Ⓓ

4 Which of the following is NOT a benefit gained from membership in a customs union?

(A) Economies of scale through larger market size   (A)

(B) Monopolies are likely to be regulated by competition from the firms of other member countries   (B)

(C) There are more benefits to be gained by non-members than members of the union   (C)

(D) Increased competition may promote greater efficiency   (D)

5 The removal of trade barriers between members that results in trading with a low cost producer in the union is BEST referred to as

(A) Transfer pricing   (A)

(B) Multilateral   (B)

(C) External economies of scale   (C)

(D) Trade creation   (D)

6 All of the following are examples of economic integration EXCEPT

(A) NAFTA   (A)

(B) EU   (B)

(C) CSME   (C)

(D) OPEC   (D)

7 All of the following are benefits of economic integration EXCEPT

(A) Trade creation   (A)

(B) Economies of scale   (B)

(C) The free movement of labour   (C)

(D) Trade diversion   (D)

8 The primary purpose of economic integration is

(A) Trade liberalisation   Ⓐ

(B) Protection from competition   Ⓑ

(C) The limitation of market access   Ⓒ

(D) The independence of sovereign states   Ⓓ

9 NAFTA was implemented to remove barriers to trade between

(A) United States of America, Canada and the Caribbean   Ⓐ

(B) United States of America, Mexico and the Caribbean   Ⓑ

(C) United States of America, Canada and Mexico   Ⓒ

(D) Canada, Mexico and the United Kingdom   Ⓓ

10 Which of the following is a trade agreement for Caribbean economies ONLY?

(A) FTAA   Ⓐ

(B) CSME   Ⓑ

(C) CARIBCAN   Ⓒ

(D) Andean Pact   Ⓓ

2.3.5 International Economic Relations

1 The role of the World Trade Organization is BEST described as

(A) To settle disputes relating to international boundaries   Ⓐ

(B) To provide protectionist barriers for small states   Ⓑ

(C) To set the rules and regulations that govern world trade   Ⓒ

(D) To provide balance of payments support   Ⓓ

2 The primary role of the International Monetary Fund is to

(A) Promote exchange rate stability as a means of facilitating trade Ⓐ

(B) To monitor and rate economic performance Ⓑ

(C) To give financial advice to regional groups of countries Ⓒ

(D) To provide loans to multinational corporations Ⓓ

3 Multinational corporations have been criticised for

(A) Technological transfer Ⓐ

(B) Increasing the rate of inflation Ⓑ

(C) Repatriation of profits Ⓒ

(D) Their low rate of foreign investment Ⓓ

4 Which of the following is a benefit of globalisation to consumers?

(A) Providing skilled labour to a country Ⓐ

(B) Access to new techniques of accounting and management Ⓑ

(C) Low prices brought about by increased competition Ⓒ

(D) Hiring low skilled workers in their start-up phase of construction Ⓓ

5 Which of the following is an opportunity available to Caribbean economies as a result of globalisation?

(A) Promote exportation of local products Ⓐ

(B) Enact legislation to restrict the entry of foreign firms Ⓑ

(C) Raise the level of taxes on the profits of foreign investors Ⓒ

(D) Provide tax incentives to local firms to invest in the domestic economy Ⓓ

6 Which of the following is a disadvantage of foreign direct investment?

   (A) Market access   Ⓐ

   (B) Transfer pricing   Ⓑ

   (C) Technological transfer   Ⓒ

   (D) A source of tax revenue   Ⓓ

7 An example of foreign direct investment is

   (A) Drilling for minerals in the Caribbean by a Canadian company   Ⓐ

   (B) The organisation of cultural events in Europe and South America   Ⓑ

   (C) Debt forgiveness by developed countries   Ⓒ

   (D) Foreign aid   Ⓓ

8 All of the following are forces which give rise to globalisation EXCEPT

   (A) Communications technology   Ⓐ

   (B) The formation of trading blocs   Ⓑ

   (C) Political influence   Ⓒ

   (D) The operations of multinational corporations   Ⓓ

9 A multinational corporation is BEST defined as a firm

   (A) With owners residing in foreign countries   Ⓐ

   (B) That conducts business in the home country only   Ⓑ

   (C) With production and distribution rights in many countries   Ⓒ

   (D) Whose branded goods and services are sold worldwide   Ⓓ

Notes

Notes

Notes